DIALOGUE ON

George Santayana

DIALOGUE ON

George Santayana

James Gutmann

Horace M. Kallen

Corliss Lamont

Milton Munitz

Ernest Nagel

John H. Randall, Jr.

Herbert W. Schneider

Edited by CORLISS LAMONT

With the assistance of MARY REDMER

HORIZON PRESS   NEW YORK   1959

The transcription of an informal evening of reminiscences and personal impressions of George Santayana (1863–1952). The discussion was led by Professor Horace M. Kallen, of the New School for Social Research, at the New York home of Dr. Corliss Lamont, Columbia Lecturer in Philosophy, who has edited the manuscript. Also participating were Columbia Professors James Gutmann, Ernest Nagel, John H. Randall, Jr., and Herbert W. Schneider; and Professor Milton Munitz of New York University. Mary Redmer assisted with the editing.

DIALOGUE ON

George Santayana

LAMONT

I thought it might be worth-while for those of us who have known George Santayana to some extent, or had some contact with him, to meet and talk; and I was very glad to be able to get Horace Kallen to join us for the evening. I came across this little book on Harvard the other day, *College in a Yard,* edited by Brooks Atkinson; and there's a paragraph in here by Horace about Santayana, just one paragraph, in which he says that after class at Harvard he used to walk out with Mr. Santayana, asking him questions, and that that very quickly built up into teas and drinks and so on. Well, this is really a very enticing passage, and it seems to me that we might carry on from there, Horace, and go back to Harvard, where you were assistant to Santayana for several years, and see if you can recover some of those impressions.

KALLEN

It began really before I became his assistant, because I encountered him first as a freshman. You know Massachusetts Hall—as it was, not as it is. We sat on very long, rough benches, facing a small platform with a desk on it. The first time I saw Santayana, I saw a very dapper figure—carrying a bowler hat, gloves and cane.

He walks in almost unnoticed, seats himself at the desk while the usual classroom rustle and noises continue, hardly subsiding. Then he begins to talk.

There is something in the voice, and something in the way he doesn't look at you. He never looked at you. I found out later he was terribly nearsighted. There was a turn of the eye that made you think of religious pictures. I finally got to see him as a sort of Murillo madonna with a mustache—a stereotype.

Usually with lectures, even the best, there comes a time when you're bored. Students wriggle in their seats, move their hands, rustle their feet, make other noises. Not, however, these Freshmen in Philosophy 1-A. You listen and look, even if you don't agree. Three or four weeks after the course began, I couldn't contain myself any longer. The things that were said were challenging, and somewhat controverted things I'd learnt from my father; so I stepped up to the desk and asked Santayana some questions. The answers took us across the yard and over to Harvard Square. That peripatetic talk started a whole series. I wasn't living in Cambridge. When I was an undergraduate, the Yard was a place for buildings such as Massachusetts, Harvard or Seaver Halls, not a field of student life.

Coming back, this course was Philosophy 1-A, "History of Ancient Philosophy," and he used to alternate with George Herbert Palmer. When he got it the first term, Palmer would give Modern, and the following year Santayana would give Modern and Palmer would give Ancient. It would go on like that. This was 1902–03.

Santayana simply had an allure. It wasn't merely the voice; it was the way he addressed you. He talked pretty much as he wrote, and he wrote pretty much as he talked. Before I knew it, I was following him around. He had a noon course on Saturday, and he'd usually go to a football game, if there was a football game. It was across at Soldiers Field. I never had time to go to the game, but once he had a ticket for me, though I couldn't use it.

During my undergraduate years he was living on Brattle Street. It's an old house, now being used partly as a restaurant and partly as a place for the sale of I-don't-know-what—*objets d'art* supposedly. He had two rooms. Medici prints hung over the mantelpiece of the fireplace. And on his desk he had a couple of bowls filled with sand and in those bowls two long goose quills.

The goose quills fascinated me and absorbed my attention for a long time. I wondered what they meant. I discovered afterwards that they had been instruments of writing at Oxford when he was there, and he had carried them along; they had become a kind of antique in his house which he didn't use any more. He wrote with a pencil.

And one day I asked him why he'd kept the quills. He pulled them out and threw them in the fireplace. Apparently something had broken with the question.

I think I took about every course that Santayana gave while I was an undergraduate. And they involved the history of philosophy, Greek philosophy —Greek philosophy at Harvard was a wonderful, exciting thing. He was then preparing *The Life of Reason;* and the course out of which it grew was called the Philosophy of History. It was given afternoons in Harvard Hall; we went up a flight of stairs, the side stairs—still standing. The platform was much higher than in Massachusetts Hall, and so he was raised very much above the audience. It was rare for a class to applaud at the end of a lecture, but usually once a week there would be a spontaneous outburst of applause.

He took my notes at the end of this two-term course; and as I had made side remarks and decorations, as well as recordings of what was said, I was a little disturbed; but they came back with pleasant comments. When I got through, I went to Princeton, and he went off also; the same two years that I was going to Princeton he was in Europe. And it was the first year, in 1904, that the first volume of *The Life of Reason* came out: *Reason in Common Sense*. The other volumes were produced soon after at intervals. He came back in 1906, and I, having been more or less kicked out of Princeton, came back too. Naturally I gravitated in his direction.

In the interval Emerson Hall had begun to function. (Emerson Hall was set up in 1903.) There he was in the modern classroom way down in front, waiting for students to come to talk to him. I somehow recognized the back, the posture, the character of the head; but when he turned around, there was a beard. A beaver. And the type of expression, the character and quality of the man were changed; there was something strange that didn't belong. He didn't carry that beard for more than half a term, but in the interval Denman Ross, who was a great master of science—though perhaps not of the art of painting—made a portrait of him with the beard, the derby, the gloves and the stick. I don't know what has become of that portrait. It may be hanging in Emerson Hall, alongside Mrs. Riebers's collocation of James, Palmer and Royce; but I am not sure. For a long time Ross kept it at home. He was doing it in some particular Spanish style, I think he said in the manner of Velasquez. It would be difficult to identify now, except that every time I think of that portrait there is something about the New England judgment of Santayana in it; and that judgment was not friendly. It was admiring but dubious; and he felt it very much.

The kind of people that were around him I never could make much of. There was Pierre La Rose. Did you know him, Corliss? Was he there in your time?

LAMONT

No, I didn't know him.

KALLEN

Well, he was a kind of precious Copeland. He was Copey with the kind of difference that ladylike manners and attitudes made. And he used to court Santayana a good deal. He was around, and there were undergraduates who were on the *Advocate* and the *Monthly* in those early days when I was living in a settlement house in Boston; I remember one time when a group of us were all there together and he brought out this jug of Glengarry whisky. He had a wonderful taste in whisky that he must have acquired at Oxford.

This jug was a long, narrow, very impressive

vessel from which to pour. You couldn't pour, except with a sort of ritual control. A heady-to-handle
—it's an Irish whisky, and I've looked for it since;
and it just isn't. La Rose got very hoity-toity about
the form of it, and I remember the embarrassment
with which Santayana tried to stop him. He changed
the conversation, somehow.

Well, then—the walks across the Yard, walking
sometimes to Roslindale where his mother lived. He
never asked me in or explained. His mother was
very old and wasn't seeing anybody; but I think he
didn't want anybody to see her. It was clear that he
didn't like her from the way he talked about her.
But so long as she lived he was a devoted son, and
at least once a week he would be going down there.
And if there were questions to discuss, on most occasions I would walk down with him.

Well, that's the undergraduate story. When I
came back, the choice between taking a degree in
English and taking a degree in philosophy was
never a true choice because all my preferences were
weighted. On the one side you had Santayana, and
you had William James, then Hugo Münsterberg,
and in a lesser way you had Josiah Royce. And in
an entirely negative way you had Palmer. On the

other side you had Kitty—Kittredge—and George Baker and Barrett Wendell (I wasn't doing much with Barrett Wendell at the time) and a lot of philologists I didn't care about particularly. So I naturally decided for philosophy when the Department offered me a fellowship, and the Department of English didn't.

That year I became Santayana's assistant and stayed there until I left for Wisconsin. He really got me the job at Wisconsin.

When his mother died he shook the dust of Cambridge and New England and the United States off his feet. No matter what inducements were offered him to return, he wouldn't return. I think Wendell Bush * at one time tried to get him to come back. Bush had a great admiration for him. Whenever he and Mrs. Bush came to Cambridge there would be a course on "Three Philosophical Poets"—and I think he did repeat the course at Columbia as well as at Wisconsin.

I remember a talk shortly after, by a fellow named Lightner Witmer, or Whitman, a professor of psychology at the University of Pennsylvania,

---

* Professor Wendell T. Bush taught in the Columbia Philosophy Department from 1905 to 1941.

one of those fathers of connectionism or naive behaviorism, who published a magazine, one number of which was devoted entirely to the denunciation of the Harvard Department of Philosophy and Psychology. And he summed up Royce as an exponent of obscurantism, James as an exponent of occultism and Münsterberg as a bluff. And of course we were talking about it and Santayana said, "I suppose he didn't regard Palmer and me as important enough, or he would have said, 'drivel and atheism.'"

Well, that's all that I think of. . . .

LAMONT

How do you explain, Horace, Harvard's attitude toward Santayana, which has always been less friendly and less sympathetic than Columbia's, for instance? And I think that holds true even today.

KALLEN

Well, he had been brought up as a Catholic. The sister—who to a very great degree was an actual mother to him and to whom he was bound in a very intense way, much more so than to his mother whom he clearly didn't like—was a devout Catholic; and even when he was already going to the Latin School, he used to be taken to mass and what-not. And they went around not far from where they lived to Boston College where there was this Catholic emphasis. Now Catholicism in Cambridge and in Boston and New England was identified with shanty Irish. It had no form or grace, nothing of the Latin quality about it; and it went also with corrupt politics and all the rest.

The anti-Catholic tradition which was much older than Santayana's generation regarded the presence of the perceptual Catholicism as somehow a carrier of evil. And then I suspect that his sister's father, Sturgis (whom his mother had married in the Philippines) and her family, which was a good stable New England family, carried a kind of resentment which could easily have become part of the social atmosphere. And as Beacon Hill and that part of Cambridge were close together, Santayana was marginal to it.

You must start with a certain detachment and feeling of aliency that he always had, always manifested, a kind of distant all-is-warm quality, a banked warmth. He was so tremendously kind to students and in fact he often scolded me for being too hard on them in section meetings and in grading exams. But that was like an aristocrat's kindness; it was largesse; it wasn't a free gift in most cases; and that kind of thing is extremely attractive to certain temperaments and very disturbing to others.

Well, in the development of the academic scene he worked essentially, I would say, from what you might call Catholic or pre-Catholic premises. The Greeks, the Greeks fundamentally, caught his concentration while he was at Oxford, working on Greek philosophy. His tutor was Henry Jackson, one of the chief people who contributed to dating Platonic dialogues, if I remember correctly.

There was always this social distance between him and the whole of New England. Then he became suspect, of course, as a critic of the genteel tradition. In the Spanish War he was definitely sympathetic to the Spanish interest without complete commitment to it. In fact he had some verses about Spain and America, if I remember correctly, that would indicate that he had a certain indignation. And the social distance spread as his philosophy developed, and the glamour that it had for certain types of undergraduate minds. Less graduate, more undergraduate. The graduates all went for Royce or for James. More for Royce than for James. They went very little for Santayana. They took courses with him; but it was only to have had a course with Santayana rather than to understand his thought and how he was thinking—*that* was philosophically condemned. So he lived in a miserable way all the time.

He was pursued by ladies from Beacon Hill and Cambridge. There was Mrs. Toy, for example. Professor Toy was from the South, and he had a much younger wife who was also a Southern belle, and she was very, very pleasant.

At a tea party after Santayana had moved to an apartment, Prescott Hall, on Cambridge Street—there were a Mrs. Winslow, Mrs. Toy and some other lady from Beacon Hill, some young undergraduate poet, myself—I think there was another person, another man, but I can't remember who it was. Santayana was giving us tea; and you got the sense of an adoration of a matinee idol that was in these women's attitudes, and Mrs. Toy's concern was apparent; but that didn't mean that a Southern belle coming up into Cambridge should be interested in a Spanish cavalier. All this had nothing to do with the attitude of authentic Cambridge or authentic Boston. He was basically an outsider.

LAMONT

In the volume of Santayana's letters * there are a number which were sent to Mrs. Toy. He is supposed to have written more letters to her than to any other single person.

KALLEN

That can very well be. There's a lady that William James wrote more letters to than he wrote to his wife. I've forgotten her name, but she is in the letters of William James † that Ralph Perry edited.

RANDALL

Well, that's natural; it's more important to *talk* to his wife.

[*Laughter*]

KALLEN

I think his wife talked to him.

[*Laughter*]

MUNITZ

What sort of courses did Santayana give on the

---

* *The Letters of George Santayana*, edited by Daniel Cory, 1955.
† *The Thought and Character of William James*, by Ralph Barton Perry, 1935.

graduate level? Were they very much different from those on the undergraduate level?

KALLEN

If you mean were they deeper and more detailed, yes. Were they different in form? No.

MUNITZ

And the subject matter?

KALLEN

There was a seminar in Aristotle, for example, that was more limited in subject matter; also a discussion of Locke, Berkeley and Hume on occasion; but he wasn't interested in that kind of thing very much. He wasn't interested in straight historic courses on the exposition of special thinkers. And I don't recall in the catalogues anything like the subjects usually offered as a rule in graduate courses in philosophy.

NAGEL

Horace, did he give courses corresponding to *The Life of Reason*?

KALLEN

He called it "The Philosophy of History."

NAGEL

Did that cover —?

KALLEN

That became *The Life of Reason.*

NAGEL

Including the fifth volume? *

KALLEN

Including the fifth volume.

NAGEL

I forget where, but there is a story that when Santayana came to write the fifth volume he was so distressed with the idea of having to write on that subject that he apparently suffered acutely.

MUNITZ

That's the legend.

KALLEN

Well, now, it could be because it meant abstract-

* *Reason in Science,* 1925.

ing from the over-all perspectives this special detail. The division into volumes was a literary device that didn't take form in the lectures at all. The reorientation was different, of course.

SCHNEIDER

Well, the first volume didn't fit into the philosophy of history, did it? Or did he put that in?

KALLEN

I think it began with a discussion of the nature of history, if I remember correctly, and then moved into the subject of what common sense means, rather than the term "reason and common sense." I had a feeling after the books began to appear that there was a considerable distance between the material of the lectures and the material of the book. And someday I am going to find my notebook, if it hasn't been lost or destroyed; and if I can handle the labor and live long enough, it will be entertaining to compare the lectures and the books.

SCHNEIDER

You don't know that Santayana wrote *Reason in Common Sense* first, do you?

KALLEN

I don't know. I know it was published first.

RANDALL

Did he himself lecture from notes?

KALLEN

He had in his pocket a piece of paper; and every so often he would peer down very close. And then he would talk. I couldn't see that the notes amounted to much. I think they were suggestions. When he started talking, the pattern seemed to be spontaneous and to develop of itself.

RANDALL

Then any notes that were preserved couldn't be reconstructed?

KALLEN

None that I know of.

LAMONT

But he talked, you say, the way he wrote—I mean that same beautiful style and cadenced sentences.

KALLEN

Yes, it was an astounding thing. It was perfect composition and perfect timing. He never ended a lecture in the middle the way both James and Royce did. There would be a beginning, a middle and an end.

NAGEL

Horace, coming back to *The Life of Reason* once more, I forget now where Santayana remarks that it was a sort of Hegelian phenomenology with a different general philosophical orientation. Did he give courses in Hegel?

KALLEN

Not in my time. He didn't like Hegel. He gave courses *about* Hegel which were devastating, but not *in* Hegel. Courses in Hegel were given either by Royce or by the ex-Alford Professor of Christian Morals . . .

LAMONT
Hocking?

KALLEN
William Ernest Hocking.

GUTMANN

I forget the dates of the sonnets. Was he writing his sonnets during the period while you were associated with him?

KALLEN

When he was packing up, ready to go to Europe —I'd come down for the summer; this was 1912, I think—and he was giving me a number of books— William James's *Principles of Psychology* which he inscribed to me and then I gave away to somebody who didn't like Harvard—then he gave me a set of Leopardi, and I leafed it through in Italian and I found verses, some of them translations and others his own verses in his own writing. And I thanked him for them. He said, "Oh, no, you can't have those." Those he took away, but I've got Leopardi; but I would much rather have had Santayana's verses.

GUTMANN

These were verses that never were published?

KALLEN

So far as I know, never.

GUTMANN

Did that represent a negative attitude on his part?

KALLEN

No, I suspect that on one side it was an intellectual exercise like doing a crossword puzzle, and that on the other side there was some feeling, private feeling, that he didn't want to share. I couldn't even read them. He took them right away. I don't know what Cory has.*

RANDALL

I once asked Santayana why he did not write more poetry, and he answered that poetry was not congenial to the spirit of the age.

LAMONT

Some of the sonnets, I believe, he wrote when he was very young.

KALLEN

Most of the sonnets were composed while he was a student. Soon afterwards he completed *Philos-*

* Daniel Cory is Santayana's literary executor.

ophers at Court * which Cory has published, known as very entertaining drama. It would be fun for philosophers to get together and distribute the parts and read them out, because it is full of irony and wisdom. And it puts a position—you've read it, Ernest? It's a really satisfying drama. And of course, there's *Lucifer*. *Lucifer* belongs to his youth and indicates his own conflict, which was more than a conflict with doctrine, because it meant breaking with his sister and the resolution that came with it.

NAGEL

What was Santayana's attitude towards your reforming zeal?

KALLEN

He tolerated it. He thought that I was wasting a scholar's time, but he could understand that I might do it to make a living.

RANDALL

Was he especially close to anybody on the Harvard faculty?

* Included in *The Poet's Testament*, 1953.

KALLEN

I can't recall any single person except Pierre La Rose; and he wasn't close to La Rose; La Rose wanted to be close to him. Quite another thing. Or Bag Fuller [B.A.G. Fuller]. Fuller was for a while a genuine disciple of Santayana's. Was he still there when you were there, Corliss?

LAMONT

He wasn't teaching, I think, but I somehow got to know him. He was around.

KALLEN

He must have been around—

LAMONT

And he went to the West.

KALLEN

He went to—of all places—the Methodist Institution, the University of Southern California, where he formed alliances with movie people and became *the* avatar of toleration and liberty for those Methodists. They also had F. C. S. Schiller.

SCHNEIDER

Did Fuller teach at Harvard?

KALLEN

Yes, he was an assistant of Santayana's, when I was a freshman, an undergraduate.

NAGEL

Do you know what political views Santayana expressed—if any—during those years? Did he have any?

KALLEN

Well, it was not known. The talk about politics was in the Platonic and Aristotelian line; but after he had left, you know, the year before I went West, there was a young gang of whom Walter Lippmann was the head and front; and there was a Harvard Socialist Society that Lippmann headed up, and they—that whole group were great *aficionados* of Santayana. They took the course in aesthetics and so on. When Santayana went abroad, I think about 1912, the year that his mother died, we had an exchange of letters about something, and in one of those letters he said, "Well, of course you may think

you are a socialist. In this way, I'm a socialist too."
But it didn't mean socialism in the sense of a party
and all the rest. It meant a certain attitude toward
human relations, structure of government.

NAGEL
Did he know anything at all of Justice Holmes?

KALLEN
If he did, he never mentioned it to me.

LAMONT
Coming back to his relationship with Harvard,
of course he was fairly popular among some people
there. He became a member of the Delphic Club,
which was one of the main clubs of the University—

KALLEN
As an undergraduate?

LAMONT
Well, actually, no. He was taken in as a graduate
member, which was very unusual.

KALLEN
It would be, but I don't know anything about

that. I don't think that that was so much a matter of popularity as a matter of distinction, like taking in a football player.

LAMONT

Yes, yes. But what I don't understand is that the Harvard Philosophy Department over these decades hasn't come to appreciate Santayana more. I mean on an intellectual basis. There may have been the bias against him that you describe. Is it due really to the fact that they're just not sympathetic to his philosophy, and that some of us down this way are?

KALLEN

They're not particularly sympathetic to his philosophy, and yet the core of *The Life of Reason* is very close to James. But the intent was so different.

GUTMANN

In what sense are you using the word "core"?

KALLEN

I'd say the postulates of adjustment and adaptation and the relation of most of the processes of thinking to the values of living. It seems to me that what Santayana absorbed from James's *Psychology* * was that mind emerged as a biological function in the struggle for survival. The whole conception of the life of reason not as a development of self-mastery or a mastery of the world around you, but a *vita contemplativa,* comes much later than the birth of intelligence. Santayana was James's pupil and psychology was in the making, you see; the whole thing was in its early stages, in process; and what came out afterwards was a new direction. It was the perversion, you might say, of the pragmatic spirit of the Catholic value system.

On the personal side, James had befriended Santayana as he had befriended so many of us. Santayana always talked about him with a kind of malicious reverence. He felt indebted, he liked him, and yet he resented him.

SCHNEIDER

Well, I'd always imagined that Santayana's playing with pre-rational, rational, and post-rational was a working over of James's *Psychology.*

* *The Principles of Psychology,* by William James, 1890.

KALLEN

Yes, I believe that.

RANDALL

What was Royce's attitude toward Santayana?

KALLEN

As if he were a loving, rebellious and angry son.

MUNITZ

He did his doctor's dissertation under Royce, did he not?

KALLEN

No, a combination. The doctoral dissertation was on this German—

SEVERAL VOICES

Lotze.

KALLEN

And I am not sure whether it was Royce or James or the other man, Bowen, who had most responsibility for it. I don't know.

MUNITZ

I recall looking at the manuscript of it at Cambridge, and what impressed me among other things was something in the handwriting which was very similar to what you've described in connection with his oral delivery—namely, that there was never an erasure, never a change; and I'm quite sure that he must have written even the first draft as a perfectly finished thing.

KALLEN

I've had manuscripts of his, and there would be hardly an erasure. I had the entire manuscript of *Three Philosophical Poets*, reading it over at the time, and it was just like that. He had three manila envelopes. You took out of them yellow sheets, ruled yellow sheets, and there was that clear, precise hand which—maybe it belonged to the generation. William James had a beautiful articulate hand like that; Royce had an awful hand, and Münsterberg's was German. Palmer's hand I never saw.

GUTMANN

Did you say that *Three Philosophical Poets* was first given as a course at Harvard?

KALLEN

Yes.

GUTMANN

Certainly it must have been considerably reduced and reworked.

KALLEN

Well, you see, in a course you read the poets, you take your time. As given in the final form of lectures, it was reduced quite a bit. It had been a single-term course, a half-course it was called.

NAGEL

Did you ever feel the obvious disdain that Santayana shows in his published writings toward the Hebraic tradition?

KALLEN

No, not at all. This question comes up every so often, Ernest; and it comes up in connection not only with Santayana, but with T. S. Eliot, and Barrett Wendell, and other close friends of mine. Now I think there's a distinction to be made. Santayana's condemnation of what he called the Hebraic tradition was part and parcel of the intellectual rejection of a world of flux and change and drama and salvation, in favor of the well-ordered Hellenic world. It had nothing to do with living Jews as such. As it happened, you know, most of the students who were meaningful to him and to whom he was meaningful, were Jews. And his—

RANDALL

They're not so close to the Hebraic tradition these days.

[*Laughter*]

KALLEN

Well, most of them were evidently—quite evidently—un-Hebraic. I wasn't. With Eliot, the same thing. The same way with a whole certain aspect of the New England generation that became very disturbed about immigration, and condemned types, while loving people. Jewishness is a sin, but you love the sinner.

GUTMANN

You mentioned the furnishings of his first rooms. Besides the goose quills, you spoke of some pictures, pre-Raphaelite. Were they his own selection?

KALLEN

They were pre-Raphaelite. They were his own selection. An English firm that made prints got them out—the name escapes me. They were very common, they were much in use at the time. Not Rossetti prints; *Medici* prints.

GUTMANN

I was interested in their significance as objects of his choice.

KALLEN

They were significant, yes. Catholic. A triptych. I don't remember now what the theme was. I have simply the image of the picture over the fireplace.

GUTMANN

I know less probably than the rest about his particular tastes and enthusiasms with respect to painting or other works of art.

KALLEN

Well, he didn't have much art work when he was

living in Rome. Did you ever go to his rooms at the Bristol, Herbert?

SCHNEIDER

Yes, but—

KALLEN

Did he ever say to you, "Well, you know, this is a hotel room, like a cocotte's"?

[*Laughter*]

I went up there, and he dug out of the bottom drawer of his bureau the medal for literature that Robert Bridges had gotten for him in England; it was quite a big, notable thing. And then somebody told me that when Mussolini was inviting contributions for the Ethiopian war Santayana contributed that, and it turned out to be gilt!

GUTMANN

I'm glad to hear it was that. Someone said it was the Butler Medal.*

NAGEL

Horace, on the one occasion when I did see him,

---

* A gold medal for distinction in philosophy established at Columbia by President Nicholas Murray Butler in 1915.

walking through the streets of Rome, I asked him whether he listened to any music. He said no. Now he wrote so sensitively about it. Did he listen to music when you knew him?

KALLEN

I don't remember his ever having gone to a concert or being concerned about music as an actual experience in any gathering—

RANDALL

He didn't play anything?

KALLEN

No, he didn't play any instruments. He drew; he was a very good draftsman, and made many cartoons for the Harvard *Lampoon.*

MUNITZ

He considered going into architecture.

KALLEN

One of the ironical occasions in Rome was when I was going to interview Mussolini, who had exploited the word "pragmatism" and "pragmatist" greatly through the *New York Times* and elsewhere. Mussolini was telling Americans that he was a pragmatist; he believed in action and so on; and a good many absolute idealists took it up and exploited it over here—

VOICE

Marxists took it up too.

KALLEN

The statement of Mussolini—Fascist and all the rest of it. Well, so I went to see Mussolini. *You* [*indicating Schneider*] were in Rome at that time.

SCHNEIDER

Yes, I remember when you went.

KALLEN

I went to see Mussolini, and at that time, Santayana was going to Fiesole to visit with Charles Strong * every so often. Strong had a special car made. He was paralyzed and had contraction. And so the day of the interview both Santayana and Strong came down in Strong's car, and they waited

* Professor Charles A. Strong, an American psychologist.

across from the Chigi Palace until I got out, to hear what happened. They seemed very—excited.

RANDALL

Were they surprised that you *got* out?

KALLEN

Oh, no, on the contrary.
[*Laughter*]

GUTMANN

They expected you out sooner?
[*Laughter*]

KALLEN

But they waited there, eager to hear the details. And I was a little let down by that eagerness. And they were let down by what I told them.

LAMONT

What did you tell them?

KALLEN

I told them that Mussolini didn't know what pragmatism was, that he may have seen the name in the newspaper, but didn't know what he was talking about. And I practically told Mussolini that.

SCHNEIDER

Santayana made one nasty crack about Mussolini while I was there, about the same week, I guess, that you called on Mussolini; he was full of the subject. He said, "Well, I must say Mussolini's good for these Italians. He makes them behave more like Englishmen!"

[*Laughter*]

LAMONT

Well now, why didn't Santayana ever want to set foot in America again, even though attractive offers were made him?

KALLEN

I can't say why. I don't know what was at the bottom of his heart, but I can tell you this, which may be a symptom. After we moved from 23rd Street to 12th Street, the New School,* we thought it would be a very good thing to have some significant figure, so to speak, to baptize the new habitation.

* The New School for Social Research, New York City.

And I got some people to agree to subscribe the necessary amount to bring Santayana over if he could come over. And I invited him. It was a personal matter. I made it personal. And he wrote back that he would like to come; he *would* come; but there's Harvard. (I have the letter somewhere.)

Now this was twenty years after he had left Harvard. His unwillingness to go back there seems like a neurosis, doesn't it? And I can't guess—

RANDALL

The New School isn't so very much like Harvard.

KALLEN

Had nothing to do with it. He didn't think that he could come to America without going to Harvard; therefore he wouldn't come to America.

SCHNEIDER

The reason he gave me one day when I tried to urge him to come to Columbia was that, "Well, I'd like to see America again, but if I came over, you'd make me lecture, and I don't want to lecture."

KALLEN

Well, that's another rationalization.

LAMONT

Didn't he enjoy teaching?

KALLEN

He said he didn't. And yet I don't know of any of that group, except James, who went out more—and with more openness and concern to students in communication, exchange; and he had a kind of generosity about it that seemed to me unusual in any teacher. Now whether he enjoyed this kind of thing or not—perhaps it was a form of penance. But he was very effective. Where he was effective, he was terribly effective.

MUNITZ

Was he the kind of teacher who ever made use of the Socratic technique?

KALLEN

No, he lectured. And after the lecture if you wanted to talk to him, he was there; he'd stay. And then there would often be Socratic irony. He was particularly Socratic with the athletes who were enrolled in the courses and whom he graded up when I graded them down.

RANDALL

Was he ever Socratic with Morris Cohen?

KALLEN

I don't think that Morris Cohen ever had a course directly with him.

MUNITZ

He did not.

NAGEL

Santayana was away when Cohen was at Harvard.

KALLEN

That's what I thought.

SCHNEIDER

Once Santayana told me, "I always like to associate with young people, but I don't like to have them treat me as a teacher, nor do I like to treat them as students."

KALLEN

Well, that's Socratic, isn't it?

NAGEL

Horace, the impression I've had of him was that if you did ask him a question, he would take that as a stimulus for another lecture rather than for a direct reply. I mean, the impression I had was that he perhaps was not very effective in the sort of give-and-take of discussion where the two people pretty much are equal and are trying to understand an issue or to clarify a point.

KALLEN

That was not my experience, Ernest. It may have developed as a function of his loneliness later on. When did you—?

NAGEL

'Thirty-four.

KALLEN

Oh, well, that was in Rome already. He had been fundamentally alone then for a long time, and the final feeling you got about it was that here was a lonely man whistling in the dark.

[*Pause*]

When Rachel * and I visited Strong at Fiesole, we were struck by his collection of statues of the great philosophers. I believe they were in cement; and they went all the way back to Plato and Socrates.

SCHNEIDER

I think in his last autobiographical volume Santayana spoke of Strong in a condescending manner, but it seemed to me that was unjust to his actual relation to him.

RANDALL

That's what I wanted to know.

SCHNEIDER

When I first learned to know Santayana at Paris, I wanted to see him badly, and I couldn't; he wouldn't answer the doorbell. Then I found out later. He apologized. He said, "Strong's daughter's just run away with this South American, and I owe

* Mrs. Kallen.

something to my friend. I've had to help him through this crisis." And he was very considerate.

KALLEN

Well, that he would be in any circumstance. Whenever there was a crisis or an issue, he was on the spot. He did what he felt was essential and necessary. But that has nothing to do with over-all attitudes. You see them together day in, day out for a week or so, and you get a sense of the give-and-take, and that's the sense that I got. Now this capacity of Santayana's for honorable dealing—feelings of obligation and commitment—was very strong in him. So far as I'm concerned he was not only a teacher whom I got to love—there was that quality about him of allure and so on—but he was a real sustaining benefactor.

One time I got sick in Cambridge and I had to go to the infirmary—very lame—and a number of undergraduates were there, including Lippmann; and up comes Santayana to see me. Now it's an unheard-of-thing, you know, at Harvard, that a teacher should come to visit a pupil like that. And actions of that kind run through the record, and those are quite different from everything that appears in the formal projection of the man. The true image of the man is in the novel, *The Last Puritan*. It's not in the auto-biographical stuff, which is a shield and a deception really.

NAGEL

Well, your remark about his attitude toward Strong struck me as being true of actually every person that he wrote about in these autobiographies—that everybody was an instrument to him.

SCHNEIDER

Yes, but as I said, that wasn't quite true of him.

KALLEN

No, no, not true of him. He had to shut them out; he had to establish his independence and the sovereignty of the soul, so to speak. This dweller in the eternal. It seemed to me the most pitiful remark that probably had ever come from him or from any philosopher who was as disillusioned as he, to say, "I live in the eternal," which was in an interview somebody had with him after the war. And my final feeling about him was that he was a lonely and yearning person who had to defend himself against his own emotions and so on, and that he built these structures.

RANDALL

Did he have to be lonely?

KALLEN

Well, I don't think it was from choice—

RANDALL

No, but I mean—

KALLEN

It seemed to me that when you take the personal history and you get the feel of the familial relations —an unloved child of a late marriage with an enormous distance of years between himself and sister; and the mother, the mother to whom he wasn't anything that she could be concerned about—you get the image of him in isolation and alone, as off in a corner, drawing by the lamp, and nobody paying any attention to him. This seems to me the projection of the entire concentration of his experience. Now if he had met, at the time he went through the Latin School and beyond, people with other atti-

tudes and other dimension, maybe the whole di-
athesis would have changed. But he got set on that
gradient, and he started building defenses against it.

GUTMANN

Will you explain what you mean in speaking of
the autobiography as a *deception*?

KALLEN

Self-deception, and maybe a deception of others
too. Maybe also a revenge on the world.

GUTMANN

There is a sentence—I think I can quote it exactly—that's always puzzled me. If I'm not mis-
taken, it's the first sentence of the last chapter in
the third volume,* in which he says, "The world is
peopled by persons and places." There are such
wonderful descriptions of places in that volume:
Cambridge, Rome, stand out. But I think perhaps
persons were to him of the same species as places essentially. I don't know whether that's saying something different from what you said in speaking of
them as instruments. At least, Ernest generalized the

* *My Host the World*, 1953.

term, "instruments." You, Horace, applied it just to Strong. Did Santayana lack interest in personality?

KALLEN

I tried to see him in contact and communication in the course of daily life, and I decided he had this, a present and warm interest, though a little detached. I think that the formulations are defensive rather than descriptions.

RANDALL

Well, in connection with Strong, for example, this business in the autobiography about Strong not having any students. As a matter of fact I had occasion to go through the records, and the number of students in each class was given in the records during the 'nineties; and Strong had about five times as many students as Cattell, for example, all during that—

KALLEN

Yes, yes. Now, how Santayana comes to the conclusion that Strong didn't have any students—he may not have had many followers; that's what he may have meant.

SCHNEIDER

Well, I may have read some of my own feelings into their feelings; but Strong had such delightful parties up there in Fiesole, and Santayana seemed to enjoy them very much. He went up there quite frequently and had delightful conversations and tea. When Strong came to Rome, they'd go out in his car on the Via Appia because Strong enjoyed reading the Latin inscriptions; and Santayana seemed to enjoy them too. He took me along a few times.

KALLEN

Did he take you along as a participant? Was he participating or did he go along, much as a nurse goes along with small children she looks after?

LAMONT

What year was that, Herbert, when you saw so much of him?

KALLEN

It was '26, wasn't it, Herbert?

RANDALL

In the summer of '26; we were over there and met you. You'd just gone there.

SCHNEIDER

Well, I remember one of the first times I'd met him, while I spent that winter in Rome. We had a regular tea date every Wednesday afternoon. And it became perfectly mechanical as far as the physics of it went. We had our tea in the Via Veneto, and then we'd walk to the Pincio and end up in the café of the Pincio, look out at St. Peter's at sunset, and walk back; and it was a regular routine with him which I enjoyed very much, but it became quite a routine. Well, at one of the first tea parties we had, I happened to have Will Durant's *The Story of Philosophy*, which had just come out; and I showed Santayana the diagram in which he had been put right after Herbert Spencer; and his eyes opened big, and he said, "Well! That fellow has real perception!"

[*Laughter*]

And he was evidently very much pleased. He said, "That's where I belong—I can see it, and that's where I'd like to be."

RANDALL

Well, now Montague *—Montague said that

---

* Barnard Professor of Philosophy William Pepperell Montague, Harvard Class of 1896.

during the Nineties when he was at Harvard the students all regarded Santayana as a kind of Spencerian.

SCHNEIDER

Well, Santayana reminisced a little then. He said, "I can't be an American; and I can't be a Spaniard, and I haven't any interest in Spain because my socialist Spain is gone. I think that as a matter of duty perhaps I should end my days in Biarritz maybe, but it doesn't appeal to me. So the best I can do, I think, is to go down as an Englishman. And I regard my stay at Oxford as a real residence; and if I go down in history at all, I'd like to go down not as a philosopher but as a man of letters. And I'd like to go down as the last of the Victorians." And I believe this reference to Spencer suggested this theme to him.

KALLEN

Yes, perhaps.

SCHNEIDER

He mentioned that several times.

RANDALL

Did that attitude towards England come out when you met him?

KALLEN

Yes, that was present all the time. I went to England as much because of him as because of James.

MUNITZ

Was that about the time he wrote "The Unknowable" for the Herbert Spencer Annual Lecture?

SCHNEIDER

No, that was later.

LAMONT

But it's interesting that he regarded this as one of the best things he ever wrote.

SCHNEIDER

While I was in Rome he wrote that little volume, *Platonism and the Spiritual Life.* And he said, "I thought it high time that somebody took the unction out of spirituality."

[*Laughter*]

KALLEN

It's still high time!

SCHNEIDER

He left a lot of it in. Then one day I was much surprised. He said, "At last I'm working on a novel! And I know the first sentence. The first sentence will be, 'Oliver's mother thought he was very unfortunate in his father.'

[*Laughter*]

"And Oliver's my hero, and I think I'll call it *The Ultimate Puritan*.* I mean the dialectically ultimate Puritan, because he's a man who very conscientiously believes he shouldn't have a conscience. And that's my predicament. And I have a double story here. This Mario is the man I think I ought to be, but I can't help liking Oliver; and that's the trouble."

So he talked to me; he went on a little with the plot and narrated a few scenes which he thought were really humorous (I couldn't see the humor); but it was very obviously autobiographic.

KALLEN

And far more authentic than the autobiographi-

* Santayana's novel, *The Last Puritan*, was published in 1935.

cal books. Partly because he assumes that it's disguised.

SCHNEIDER

Then a little later he began talking about the life of Christ. He said, "I think I'd like to write a life of Christ before I die; and if I do, I'll start the life of Christ with the Mount of Transfiguration; that's where it begins." And he did a little of that in his *Idea of Christ in the Gospels*. But that idea he played with for many years, I know. And he played with the *Dominations and Powers*, as he called it; but he said he never would publish that.*

[*Laughter*]

KALLEN

The roots of it were already in *The Life of Reason*.

NAGEL

Was his memory as good as he pretended when he recalls all the courses that he had and the various dinners that he had 20 years before? I think it was really remarkable.

* The book was published in 1951.

RANDALL

When I saw him, he said he was very much afraid that his memory was going, and he couldn't write anything sustained any more.

SCHNEIDER

By the time he wrote his autobiography, his memory was certainly going.

KALLEN

It was a good memory, but only for so much; it apparently had ceased to be so.

LAMONT

About his loneliness, he chose, after all deliberately, after he went to Europe—didn't he?—to lead a rather isolated life. That is, he was glad to see people, Americans who came by once in a while, and he played around with Strong; but then he did choose to be alone most of the time; and if he was lonely, didn't he pretty much enjoy it?

KALLEN

He didn't make any effort. He didn't resist companionship if it offered itself, but I doubt whether he had the will or the hunger for it.

RANDALL

When did he stop going back to Spain and Avila?

KALLEN

Oh, that was long before he had settled in Rome. When I saw him, his sister was still alive in Avila.

RANDALL

When did she die?

KALLEN

I think she must have died in the early 'thirties.

RANDALL

Well, he didn't go back after that?

KALLEN

No, he didn't go back at all after that. And he didn't like his brother-in-law.

RANDALL

No.

SCHNEIDER

When I first knew him, he didn't give me the impression so much of loneliness as simply of seclusion. He said, "I don't have to travel and see the world because enough of the world comes to see me. But as for the Italians, there's a problem. You see, the only Italian I allow to visit me is Vivante." * (I don't know whether that was true or not, but at least that's what he told me.) He said, "I must keep my distance from the Italians; otherwise I'd be swamped with them; so I purposely seclude myself from the Italians, but I have enough visitors to give me a sociable time." He didn't seem to mind it.

KALLEN

Well, I think you can be unsecluded and lonely, and secluded and lonely. You see, what you shut out is one thing, but what you want and don't get is another. And it's difficult to say what Santayana wanted, what kind of emotional security was involved. One thinks back to the mother and sister all the time. But of course you can be profoundly imposed upon by too much company and get lonelier and lonelier.

RANDALL

Did he, with all these people who went to see

* Professor of Philosophy Leone Vivante of Siena.

him and to whom he made these various remarks, always play a part?

KALLEN
I am sorry?

RANDALL
Was he always playing a part?

KALLEN
I don't have an image of his playing a part— more of his making the effort of a correct host.

RANDALL
Oh, he did that very much.

KALLEN
Yes.

RANDALL
But I meant on the intellectual side.

KALLEN
He was trying to meet the challenge—if there

was one—on the intellectual side. That was part of his hospitality. But I don't think he cared—and I think that what he was saying was so often incidental to his fundamental attitudes and thinking, a kind of soliloquy out loud. That's where you get this notion that he wasn't responsive. When he *was* like that, you might often get the feeling that he was shutting out conversation, real contact, with the person to whom he was talking at length.

SCHNEIDER

I had only one disagreeable experience along that line with him. Usually in conversation he was not only open and affable, but he himself seemed to enjoy it. The conversation was—oh, about all sorts of things—but it was always a literary conversation.

KALLEN

Well, he liked you, Herbert; he liked you.

SCHNEIDER

My wife and I were together at these tea parties with Santayana; but one day I wanted to talk the doctrine of "essences" to him, and I really wanted to find out what he would say to my criticism of his doctrine of essences. So I urged Carol not to come with me that time, to let me go alone; and I showed up alone. And he said, "Why isn't Mrs. Schneider with you?" And I said, "Well, she couldn't come to-day." Then he was a little disgruntled; but we walked to the Pincio, and as we walked I started giving him a lecture on the subject of essences, and telling him I thought there was a big difference between essences in sense experience, and *conceptual* essences. He didn't seem to see the point at all, so I repeated it; and he seemed awfully stupid. And I got tired of repeating it, and he finally said, "Yes, I've heard of concepts—

[*Laughter*]

"But what of it?" And I shut up; he didn't say anything more.

KALLEN
Yes, he did not like sermons.

SCHNEIDER
No, he didn't.

LAMONT
Well, when I saw him in Rome in 1950 I got the

same impression as you, Herbert, about his leading a secluded life. He was very pleasant to me, and our talk was pretty much technical philosophy subjects for two afternoons, and I couldn't help wondering whether what I would call his chosen seclusion was in his own mind in order that he might continue this tremendous output of great philosophical work. Or don't you think he thought in those terms?

KALLEN

I don't think he did. I don't think he had a plan or project after *The Life of Reason*. I think occasions provoked him to expression; and then, when he went at it, he went at it in one continuous swoop. His mode of writing indicates a kind of slow pattern of continuity of thinking; and most of the things that he has to say after *The Life of Reason*—when they're not social, not like *Soliloquies in England* or *Character and Opinion in the United States*—are like *The Realm of Essence, The Realm of Matter*, and so on; they're re-statements, as independent variables, of things that have a quite different meaning and color when they come together in the total stream.

LAMONT

Oh, yes, but he kept on writing and producing. You said he didn't have any plan, but he certainly kept going all that—

KALLEN

Yes. The man had no companions, he talked to himself. He talked to himself with a pen. And fortunately he had a publisher, Scribner's, who was ready to publish what he sent.

SCHNEIDER

But he gave me the impression, in Rome at least, that he had to work every morning. He called it work, and he didn't talk as though he enjoyed writing. But he had to do his work in the morning, and in the afternoon he was free. But he used to give me the impression that he worked hard every morning.

MUNITZ

I've been trying to say there certainly was a plan when he wrote that essay on "Some Meanings of the Word *Is*"; he certainly had the nucleus, pattern of the whole realm of essence, and it took him many years to—

KALLEN

Well, he had had that for a long time. It's implicit even in the *Sense of Beauty*.

VOICES

Yes, yes.

MUNITZ

Professor Kallen, would you say that on the whole the main ideas of the later works were already there and significant for him in the earlier ones?

KALLEN

I think they were implicit. I think that fundamental changes or alterations didn't take place; I think there were shifts of emphasis; but that there's a continuous movement, an unbroken one, from the first positions in *The Life of Reason* to the last one in *The Realm of Essence, Realm of Matter, Realm of Spirit*.

MUNITZ

He had some very strong reservations about *The*

Life of Reason in what he had to say towards the end of his life; in looking back on it he thought it was rather poor.

KALLEN

Well, of course, having become something that had entered the tradition, he had to reject it.

SCHNEIDER

Yes. But he gave me the impression once of feeling as though he were starting something new. After *The Realm of Essence* appeared, one day he was really bubbly—effervescent—and said, "Well, I've got a toy now, and I like to play with it. At last I've got a system, and I play with my system like a child." But that seemed to him then to be something brand new, as a system. I don't know whether it was, but I know he talked that way.

KALLEN

I wouldn't know. I don't myself get the feel of anything brand new, but you know you get a—just a new feeling of the same thing, and from your own inner perception it may be brand new, and to everybody else it may be stale.

He could be gay and cheerful and un-malicious, and then all at once there would be a sideswipe at the prey, like a cat at somebody; and it would haul you up short.

LAMONT

He worked every morning while you were in Rome, Herbert, and then he relaxed in the afternoon. Did you ever see him in the evening?

SCHNEIDER

No, I don't think he had evenings. Or I don't remember. He would eat in a restaurant—he had a few favorite restaurants. I had a few dinners with him, but then he would—

SCHNEIDER and KALLEN

Go to his room afterwards—

KALLEN

Undress, bathe and read.

SCHNEIDER

He might have read in the evening what he wrote in the morning. I wouldn't be surprised. Towards the end when I think he began to show his age a little—I hadn't seen him for a long while—he said, "Oh, you're from Columbia!" I said yes. "Well, you fellows from Columbia will never understand me. You still talk about me as a naturalist, and I'm *not* a naturalist." And he was quite insistent, and he blamed us as a group—

RANDALL

Well, he took that line with me of course too, and I've never been able to find out how seriously he meant that. He said, "I *hate* nature!"

GUTMANN

That was just what you called, before, "putting on an act," Jack; and I wonder how seriously one *can* take all these things. Deception comes in, even self-deception. There is one sentence in the Schilpp volume * in which he couples Irwin Edman and Milton here and someone else.

MUNITZ
Vivas?

* *The Philosophy of George Santayana*, edited by Paul A. Schilpp, 1940.

SCHNEIDER

Sterling Lamprecht, I think.

MUNITZ

No, Eliseo Vivas.

NAGEL

No, the New York contingent.

LAMONT

Oh, he hits them very hard, doesn't he?

GUTMANN

It's more than that.

MUNITZ

And there are certain—interestingly enough there are some passages in which he dropped Vivas and just coupled Irwin and myself, and it was at that point that he made what seemed to me some remarks that had an anti-Semitic flavor. I thought that that was rather significant; and it was on that point, I believe, that Dewey commented in his review of the volume, and said that this was not becoming to a philosopher of Santayana's stature.

SCHNEIDER

I think that was a casual remark. I wouldn't take it seriously. I don't think he took that seriously.

NAGEL

These remarks of Santayana's that nobody at Columbia understood him, do you think they were his way of saying that Dewey was sort of representing Columbia and Dewey would not understand him? Santayana called himself a materialist, not a naturalist, and I think his criticism of Dewey was that he didn't really respect matter.

SCHNEIDER

Well, of course Dewey irritated him by calling him a half-hearted naturalist, you see. And he'd want to go the whole hog if he *were* a naturalist. "No," he said, "I'm a —" I don't know how he characterized it, but he meant that he had the essence of romantic idealism in him, and he was putting it in reverse.

LAMONT

Well, wasn't he aware of Dean Woodbridge's *

* Professor of Philosophy F. J. E. Woodbridge of Columbia.

appreciation? Did Woodbridge ever meet him, by the way?

SCHNEIDER
He never talked about Woodbridge.

RANDALL
So far as I know Woodbridge never met him.

SCHNEIDER
No. I made a point of telling him how much Woodbridge—

MUNITZ
Well, Woodbridge reviewed *The Life of Reason.*

SCHNEIDER
Yes, I know, but Santayana never talked about him.

LAMONT
Is it true that Santayana would get the reviews from his publishers and throw them in the wastepaper basket without reading them?

KALLEN

Yes, in my experience, it's true. The publisher would send the reviews, but he wouldn't pay any attention to them. He did pay attention to direct statements from colleagues, but not clippings.

MUNITZ

I was rather amused because it doesn't quite coincide with the remark he made in response to my sending him what was actually my first printed piece in the *Columbia Review*—when I reviewed *Obiter Scripta*, as I recall—and there was also a review by John Dewey of—now what was it?

RANDALL
The Last Puritan.

MUNITZ
And so I sent him the piece, and in reply he—

KALLEN
Did you inscribe it?

MUNITZ
I sent it.

KALLEN

Well, *personally*? Indicating that it came from you?

MUNITZ

Yes, I sent a note accompanying it.

KALLEN

That's it, that's it!

MUNITZ

I remember he thanked me for sending it to him because he "so rarely gets the opportunity of seeing reviews" that he's delighted to get evidence of some notice in print of his books!

[*Laughter*]

KALLEN

Well, that's a very different thing, Milton, from a bunch of newspaper clippings from a clipping bureau.

GUTMANN

Why? Why is it really so different? I've heard this said about others too. But—

KALLEN

Well—

RANDALL

After you had left, did he take them *out* of the wastebasket?

[*Laughter*]

KALLEN

I'll have to consult the oracle on it!

SCHNEIDER

I had one letter from him that really should be published. I sent him *The Puritan Mind,* and he apparently read a good deal of it, wrote me a long letter, said, "This book bothers me." He said something nice about it, but he said, "According to you Emerson isn't a Puritan! And you use *Puritan* quite differently from the way I do." Then he gave a definition of Puritan which was wonderful from his point of view, and of course fitted Oliver perfectly. But he regarded Emerson as the embodiment of Puritanism and said he wasn't much interested in the Puritans in the narrower sense the way I describe them. And he had a very nice paragraph on "the omnificence of God."

LAMONT

You probably have a lot of other letters from Santayana too.

SCHNEIDER

No, I have that one poem that I finally published in the *Journal,* that little poem that came out of a conversation with Strong—light verse. Then he handed me a volume of Freud with a lot of little marginal poems that were very amusing. But I haven't many letters. This is the only one that I think might be worth publishing.

LAMONT

But there are a number of letters outstanding, I judge, that weren't published in the volume edited by Cory. I just wonder what's going to happen to those—

SCHNEIDER

I would have sent him this, but I couldn't find it.

KALLEN

I have, I guess, all the letters that he'd written me, but I don't really know where they are. And when I die, I guess somebody'll either dig them out, burn them, or something.

GUTMANN
Didn't Cory plan further volumes?

LAMONT
Well, he's working on a couple—I asked Cory to come tonight incidentally, and—

SCHNEIDER
Is he here?

LAMONT
No, he said—

KALLEN
"Just invited by cable, so I could fly over; it's an overnight—"

LAMONT
He said he just couldn't make it, but he sent everybody his regards and said he would love to be here to talk about the Master. And he was working on at least two Santayana books. But he hasn't

planned, so far as I know, another volume of the letters.

Jack, didn't you visit Santayana a couple of times in Rome?

RANDALL

Yes, we were in Rome in 1934 during Easter week, and I saw him three or four times. One thing impressed me at that time, that he was most anxious to know all about the United States and what everybody thought about him there. It was hard for me to shift the conversation in other directions, and he seemed to be very much orientated towards America.

SCHNEIDER

But when Walter Lippmann came over there, you remember what he said to him?

LAMONT

No.

SCHNEIDER

Walter Lippmann went over to visit him, and he made a luncheon date with him, and apparently

Santayana forgot it. Lippmann sat a long while there waiting for him, and finally he had them telephone up to the room; and Santayana came down and apologized, said he forgot, and went in to luncheon. And he said to Walter Lippmann, "Well, has anything happened in the world that I ought to know about? You are *The World's* editor!"

[*Laughter*]

And Lippmann was rather taken aback. He said, "Why I guess not!"

NAGEL
Did Frankfurter know Santayana?

KALLEN
Frankfurter? No, I don't think so.

SCHNEIDER
Santayana enjoyed his own style. And he liked to talk about his style and the tricks of the trade.

GUTMANN
What were his relations to Eliot, if any? None?

KALLEN
Not in my time.

RANDALL

Eliot was all Bradley, of course.

SCHNEIDER

He said there was one person he liked to read very much, and that was the author of *Elizabeth and Her Garden*.

KALLEN

Oh, you mean the first Lady Russell.

SCHNEIDER

Yes.

MUNITZ

He writes about her in his autobiography.

SCHNEIDER

Yes, he said he enjoyed her humor and her writing very much.

KALLEN

Yes, *Elizabeth and Her German Garden*. And he seems to have been really fond of Bertie's older brother.*

* John Francis Stanley, Second Earl Russell.

MUNITZ

Despite the fact that the brother called him Sargent after a while and failed to remember his name!

GUTMANN

I was referring to President Eliot—I know there was some confusion—a moment ago. I think Jack meant T. S.; and there must have been at least official relations to Charles Eliot. I wondered whether there was any—

KALLEN

President Eliot? I don't know now. I have only assorted impressions of rumors and talks. He didn't approve of Santayana.

GUTMANN

I've read that. You don't know any of the facts?

KALLEN

He delayed his promotion.

RANDALL

Was Eliot at all close to any of the Harvard philosophers?

KALLEN

Oh, yes, he was a Unitarian, you know, and for his time an extraordinarily liberal and open-minded one. And usually he took recommendations if they came from the department, and he took them from James and Palmer, and perhaps in the beginning more Palmer than James. Now James wanted to push Santayana, and apparently Eliot delayed it.

LAMONT

How about Lowell? Did he have any relation with Santayana?

KALLEN

I don't know. All I know about Lowell is—oh, I know two stories about him; but I don't know whether that would indicate an attitude toward Santayana or not. One story is that somebody was talking about the various departments of Harvard, and they were discussing the Department of Philosophy and saying, "That's all hot air." And Lowell retorted immediately, "At least it's hot!"

And the second story that I know is that an overseer had suggested the appointment of a somewhat notorious liberal to Harvard in the Department of

Philosophy; and Lowell said to him, "You know at Harvard we have academic freedom, and we have to be very careful whom we appoint."

[*Laughter*]

SCHNEIDER

I got the impression that Santayana, with all his Catholicism which he liked to talk about, never went to church and didn't like church. I don't know whether he *never* went, but—

KALLEN

Well, I think he went. I think that as a schoolboy in the Latin School—

RANDALL

As a boy, a child, he—

KALLEN

As a child. And I think that when he was an undergraduate at Harvard, he went, but he went with his sister, even—or from a sense of duty, but he went.

RANDALL

He went in Avila with his family.

KALLEN

Well, that is a routine which didn't matter. It mattered to the family as the sort of thing you do.

SCHNEIDER

I happened to call on him the afternoon of the day before Christmas, and I excused myself a little early because I said I wanted to go down to Ara Coeli and see the children say their poems to the Christ child in the crib. There was quite a wonderful ceremony there on Christmas Eve. And he looked at me and he said, "Well, I'm amazed at you. You go to things like that? I call such things blushy."

KALLEN

Yes. Well, I think a lot of things that he stopped doing were operative in his memory in a variety of ways, and they get restated and transvalued in outer expression. But I should say it is not that he loved Catholicism less but that he hated Protestantism more.

LAMONT

Do you have a firm opinion, Horace, as to Santayana's place in the history of philosophy?

KALLEN

I think anybody's place in the history of philosophy is a matter of accident.

LAMONT

Well, now, you don't really believe *that*?

KALLEN

I really do believe that. Somebody gets picked up; he has vocal and persuasive disciples; a school gets set up; reports are written—they may be forgotten and lost altogether, or they may be carried on by organizations of power, the way Shakespeare is carried on, the way the Bible used to be carried on. Who reads the Bible now since the Church has lost control of education? And who would be reading Shakespeare now if there were not entrance examinations for college requiring the reading of two or three of Shakespeare's plays? The vehicles of communication and the relevancy of selected material are what makes the difference. What was Peirce's place in the history of philosophy? What was it in 1910? And then along came these kids who were sure that they knew more about Peirce than Dewey or James did, and provided the correct view of

Peirce, having edited his works; and Peirce now has a vogue. Well, why does he have a vogue? Why Plato or Aristotle or anybody? Somebody chooses to push the damn thing. The Madison Avenues of the world keep working.

LAMONT

Yes, but there has to be something to push.

KALLEN

Well, of course there's something to push. But the place is made by the pusher, not by the pushed.
[*Laughter*]

GUTMANN

Outside of current American histories of recent philosophy, does Santayana figure in historical literature of the Continent to any extent?

RANDALL

There's quite a section on him in this Abbagnano's *History of Philosophy*.

LAMONT

What nationality is he?

RANDALL

Italian.

SCHNEIDER

Well, I think one book that should go down in the history of philosophy is *Skepticism and Animal Faith*. I think it is really a historical book.

KALLEN

That appeals to you?

SCHNEIDER

Not so much because it appeals to me; it seems to me it has a place in history. That's what I was trying to suggest.

KALLEN

You're assigning it a place in history. Whether it will have the place you assign it is in the lap of the gods; and the gods have an awfully wiggly lap.

LAMONT

Well, but here you have the added quality of a remarkable literary style which is a factor in making a writer live, surely; and on this ground Santayana would presumably live longer than Dewey.

KALLEN

Then Hegel would have died long ago and
F. C. S. Schiller would have been much more alive;
Kant would never have been born; and Hume would
have signified in an extraordinary way.

SCHNEIDER

Well, from that point of view, Corliss, I think
that Santayana was right in saying that he was the
last of the Victorians, don't you? As a writer?

KALLEN

Well, I'd say I'm hopeful.

MUNITZ

In terms of his staying power as measured by
the paperbacks, at any rate at the present time, he
seems to be doing rather well. He's one philosopher
who's likely to live for a considerable time, I would
say.

KALLEN

In terms of paperbacks? How long?

MUNITZ

Well—

KALLEN

If a book, say like Will Durant's *Story of Philosophy*, becomes an accepted, widely accepted textbook in the schools, where he had reference to Santayana, Santayana would be carried by that reference. If on the other hand, Bertrand Russell's *History of Western Philosophy*—which is not so good as Will Durant's, in my judgment—is the textbook, how long do you suppose Santayana would be carried? If you have the two competing, well, you may have choices.

VOICE

Did Santayana ever say anything about Matthew Arnold that you can remember?

KALLEN

No.

LAMONT

I think that he admired Matthew Arnold's style. And I've always felt that there was a strong affinity between his conception of religion and Matthew Arnold's in *Literature and Dogma*.

SCHNEIDER

I think Arnold's *Hebraism and Hellenism* he swallowed whole, too.

KALLEN

Yes, that. For all of that Matthew Arnold was definitely the matrix in the English-speaking world.

NAGEL

My guess would be that Santayana would never appeal to people whose interest is primarily technical, that is, whose interest in philosophy is primarily technical. Of course it doesn't lend itself to that kind of emphasis.

KALLEN

Well, the translation into the language of the technicians should be an appealing task to somebody, and may so become. The chief thing is that the idiom is so different, it's another language. It's like saying that a man who writes in Greek wouldn't appeal to a man who writes in English.

SCHNEIDER

For years I liked to read and reread the *Dialogues in Limbo*. I thought that was his best writing.

KALLEN
Yes.

SCHNEIDER
But the last time I picked them up they didn't go so well. I don't know why.

KALLEN
Take them to bed with you.

SCHNEIDER
I think one of the things I like best is his chapter on Distraction in *The Realm of Spirit*.

MUNITZ
In *The Realm of Spirit*, yes.

SCHNEIDER
I didn't like the rest of the book very much, but I liked that chapter.

LAMONT
Did you see that the new paperback edition of *Dialogues in Limbo* has two new dialogues?

MUNITZ

I think an interesting question might be to consider whether Santayana was the kind of philosopher or writer who would continue to exert an influence as a philosopher if he were not made available by somebody in the academic world who, for example, would use him as a text in a course and would manage to convey something of what he thought to be the importance of Santayana. Now, for example, men like Morris Cohen or Woodbridge certainly played that role for many of us. And I'm interested in knowing whether there are any people who take Santayana, so to speak, independently of that; and I wonder whether for example in England, perhaps, one of the reasons why he is not as well known is because of the fact that he does not serve in that way as the subject matter for a course.

KALLEN

In England of course they don't have textbooks. They read in the vacations, and they listen to lectures or play around or produce essays in term, in the philosophical discipline, in the humanities courses, and so on. I don't know how it would be in the provincial universities.

SCHNEIDER

Well, I think it's unfortunate he's out of style—
from a literary point of view he's certainly out of
style now. But I imagine he'll come back.

KALLEN

He'll come back like Henry James.

SCHNEIDER

Yes, he'll come back, I'm sure.

LAMONT

I wonder how Santayana sounds in a foreign
language. I've never seen a translation myself.

KALLEN

I wonder if there's any translation of him into
Spanish, and how he would read in Spanish, because there's a kind of cadence. Curious. I think
about Conrad, and I think about Israel Zangwill,
people whose primary language was not English,
and who developed a kind of distinction of style—
quite personal—and with a color that is quite different from the color of writers whose natural and
mother tongue was English. Now Santayana really

didn't learn to speak or use English until he was nine years old. Conrad was much older. And Zangwill must have been in England but grew up in a Yiddish-speaking town.

SCHNEIDER

Where was it Santayana said his ambition was to say in good English the most un-English thing?

MUNITZ

"A Brief History of My Opinions."
[*Laughter*]

LAMONT

What do you mean, Santayana's out of style so far as literary form—?

SCHNEIDER

That kind of a style isn't popular now.

KALLEN

So far as I can see, he never was in style in this country. When I was growing up certainly the preferences were for the quick, short sharp sentence, uncadenced; and the line from O. Henry to Hemingway was the true line. In many ways you put Santayana alongside of Emerson and Henry James— not *William*, but *Henry*—and the patterning, cadence—it's like Bach, you know.

SCHNEIDER
It must have hurt Santayana that William James should have been such a literary success.

KALLEN
Well, people read William James with a certain—

SCHNEIDER
He's very much more in style.

KALLEN
Much more in style, yet Santayana's a better writer, much more controlled and patterned right. I say *control*; I don't mean the control was *in* him, but the impression is he had control.

SCHNEIDER
I think his conversation had even more sparkle than his writing.

KALLEN

The writing does not have sparkle. It has grace and smoothness. The conversation—

SCHNEIDER

But in conversation his eyes—

KALLEN

The eyes sparkled, there was that slight gurgle, that smile. The teeth flash, and then you get asides and askances, and you feel that this man is lifting curtains and dropping them. It's a kind of magic as you talk with him. That isn't present in the written thing. But what is present in the written thing is— serious. Even when he's wittiest and most malicious, it's serious.

SCHNEIDER

You know I happened to pick up his description of the occasion when he read that essay on "The Unknowable" at Oxford. He said, "The only light in the room was the light in my eyes!"

[*Laughter*]

LAMONT

Well, I wonder if you'd like to go in the dining

room and have some drinks and continue the conversation there. Unless you'd want to sum up, Horace?

KALLEN

Well, what is there to sum up?

MUNITZ

From what you said earlier.

KALLEN

The summary is the accident.

RANDALL

What would Santayana have become if he hadn't got tangled up with Boston?

KALLEN

That reminds me of Russell's question: What would have become of the history of mankind if Cleopatra's nose had been half an inch longer?

LAMONT

Yes. Suppose Santayana had taught first at Columbia?

KALLEN

Or if Santayana had grown up in Spain, as he might have. If he had written in Spanish, he could have had at least the same quality of impact as Unamuno.

GUTMANN

Doesn't he say somewhere why he chose English?

KALLEN

Why, I think he grew up into it; it became the medium of communication and expression from his ninth year.

GUTMANN

Had he lost his capacity to write Spanish?

KALLEN

He spoke Spanish; he wrote Spanish—

RANDALL

He said he couldn't write in Spanish—

KALLEN

He wrote letters to his father.

RANDALL

Yes, but I mean he wrote domestic Spanish; he couldn't write literary Spanish.

KALLEN

Yes, but had he ever tried? He didn't want to try so far as I could make out.

SCHNEIDER

I think he puts on a big façade about all the Spanish in him. I don't think he's Spanish at all.

KALLEN

No, my—

SCHNEIDER

No, he isn't Latin either, he's just a good American.

[*Laughter*]

KALLEN

My feeling—

RANDALL

Yes. I don't know whether if it hadn't been for Harvard he would have had anything.

SCHNEIDER

I don't think he's a product of Harvard.

KALLEN

I think he's much more readily assimilable to Emerson than he is to Europeans.

MUNITZ

Don't you think he's at least as Latin as Berenson?

RANDALL

The last of the Genteel Tradition.
[*Laughter*]

KALLEN

The earlier Santayana poems, in the Latin School *Register*, which he wrote when he was a boy, seem exactly like A. E. Housman's, exactly the same meter. It sounds like a proleptic parody.

SCHNEIDER

Well, talking of parodies, I have here a little philosophic parody that Santayana wrote.

GUTMANN
Is that your Santayana poem?

SCHNEIDER
Yes.

GUTMANN
Was that in the *Journal of Philosophy*? Have you printed it—?

SCHNEIDER
Yes, I put it in the *Journal*. I published it in the *Journal* a few years ago—in 1952.

VOICE
And you framed it?

SCHNEIDER
Yes, I have it framed in my office. I think it's very clever. I'll read it to you:

> *"I thought, before I learned to think,*
> *That bread was food and water drink,*
> *But now I know that drink and food*
> *Are simple phases of the good.*

My need of nourishment makes meat
Out of such things as I can eat;
Only that drink is drink in act
Which irrigates my thirsty tract;
And because I am slaked and fed
Water is water and bread bread.
Pips, bones, and gristle and the rest,
Express my failure to digest.
My mind, with all in thought comprised,
Is just digestion realized;
The whole world else, beyond all question,
Is my projected indigestion.
How came it that so bright a youth
Ever could doubt this limpid truth?
Because, concerning food and drink,
I thought before I learned to think." *

KALLEN

Philosophy in the grand manner!

* Santayana wrote this satire on subjectivism about 1926 as a comment on a paper by Professor Schneider entitled "Confessions of an Epistemological Neophyte," which made an analogy between sensation and digestion.

BIOGRAPHICAL NOTES

JAMES GUTMANN, Professor of Philosophy and Chairman of the Department of Philosophy at Columbia University, was born in New York City 62 years ago. He was educated at the Ethical Culture School, Columbia College (A.B.) and Columbia University (M.A., Ph.D.). From 1917 to 1928 he taught history and ethics in the Ethical Culture School at New York City, and during that period was managing editor of the *Ethical Standard* and associate leader of the New York Society for Ethical Culture.

A member of the Department of Philosophy of Columbia University since 1920, he is the author of *Schelling—Of Human Freedom* and *Spinoza's Ethics,* and is co-author of other books, including *An Introduction to Reflective Thinking, A College Program in Action,* and *The Philosophy of Ernst Cassirer.*

HORACE M. KALLEN, A.B., Ph.D., L.H.D., Litt.D., was born in Germany in 1882 and came to the

United States in 1887. He was educated at Harvard, Princeton, Oxford and Paris.

He was a favorite pupil of William James who left his unfinished *Some Problems of Philosophy* for Dr. Kallen to edit, and was in close contact during his service at Harvard with Santayana and Royce. He was an associate of John Dewey and F. C. S. Schiller in developing the pragmatic philosophy with which they are identified. His special interest was extending this philosophy to the arts, to education, and to religion.

His published works include *William James and Henri Bergson, The Liberal Spirit, Cultural Pluralism and the American Idea, Secularism Is the Will of God, Utopians at Bay,* and other books.

Now Professor Emeritus in the Graduate Faculty and Research Professor in Social Philosophy at the New School for Social Research, he also is Honorary President of the Conference on Methods in Philosophy, succeeding the late John Dewey.

CORLISS LAMONT, writer, teacher, and humanist philosopher, was born in Englewood, New Jersey, in 1902. He was graduated from Harvard in 1924, studied at Oxford for a year, and took his Ph.D. at Columbia in 1932. He is a member of the American Philosophical Association, the American Humanist Association, the Academy of Political Science, the NAACP, and the Clan Lamont Society of Scotland.

A fighter for the traditional freedoms in the American Bill of Rights, Dr. Lamont served for 20 years as a Director of the American Civil Liberties Union. He is now Chairman of the Bill of Rights Fund which he founded, and Vice Chairman of the Emergency Civil Liberties Committee.

His published works include *The Philosophy of Humanism, The Illusion of Immortality, The Independent Mind, Freedom Is as Freedom Does* and other books. He also edited an anthology of poetry, *Man Answers Death.* He has taught at Cornell, Harvard, and the New School for Social Research, and is now a lecturer in philosophy at Columbia University.

MILTON K. MUNITZ, Professor of Philosophy at New York University, was educated at The College of the City of New York, where he took his B.A. in 1933, and at Columbia University, where he received his M.A. in 1935 and his Ph.D. in 1939.

Out of his interest in Santayana grew Dr. Munitz's book, *The Moral Philosophy of Santayana*, as well as his contribution to another volume, *The Philosophy of Santayana*, edited by P. A. Schilpp. Other books by Dr. Munitz include *Space, Time and Creation, Theories of the Universe*, and *A Modern Introduction to Ethics*.

ERNEST NAGEL, born in Novemesto, Czechoslovakia, November 1901, was educated in New York City's public schools, The College of the City of New York, and at Columbia University, where he received his M.A. in 1925, and his Ph.D. in 1930. After teaching in the New York City schools from 1923 to 1929, he served a year as instructor in philosophy at The College of the City of New York, and since 1931 has taught at Columbia University where he has been John Dewey Professor of Philosophy since 1954.

A Guggenheim Fellow in 1934–35 and 1951–52, he is now a Fellow at the Center for Advanced Study in the Behavioral Sciences (1959–60). He is also a Fellow of the American Academy of Arts and

Sciences, and was President of the Association for Symbolic Logic (1946–48) and of the American Philosophical Association, Eastern Division, 1954. His published works include *On the Logic of Measurement, Introduction to Logic and Scientific Method* (with Morris R. Cohen), *Principles of the Theory of Probability, Sovereign Reason, Logic Without Metaphysics,* and *Gödel's Proof* (with J. R. Newman).

JOHN HERMAN RANDALL, JR. has taught philosophy at Columbia University since 1920; since 1950 he has served as F. J. E. Woodbridge Professor of Philosophy. He is author of *The Making of the Modern Mind, Nature and Historical Experience, The Role of Knowledge in Western Religion,* and other books, and has written many articles and contributions to co-operative volumes. He has served as Chairman of the Editorial Committee of *The Journal of the History of Ideas,* and as President of the American Philosophical Association, Eastern Division, and of the Renaissance Society of America. He is joint editor of *The Journal of Philosophy.*

Mr. Randall was first drawn to Santayana as an

undergraduate by the admiration and enthusiasm of his teachers, John Erskine and F. J. E. Woodbridge. Ever since he has been a careful student of Santayana's writings, and he was privileged to move in a group that eagerly recounted every scrap of information and every anecdote about the expatriate American thinker. A number of conversations with Santayana in the old Hotel Bristol in Rome brought the tang of immediacy to this long vicarious acquaintance.

HERBERT W. SCHNEIDER was born in Berea, Ohio, on March 16, 1892. He attended The College of the City of New York for one year, then studied at Columbia University, where he took his A.B. in 1915 and his Ph.D. in 1917. Also the holder of an L.H.D. from Union College (1947), Dr. Schneider has taught philosophy and religion at Columbia since 1918, and since 1956 has been a Columbia Professor Emeritus of Philosophy. In 1958–59 a Whitney Visiting Professor at Colorado College, he is now teaching at Pomona College.

During the course of his career Dr. Schneider has been a Rockefeller Research Fellow in Italy

(1926–27) ; a Fulbright Fellow in France (1950) ; and served in Paris in 1953–56 as head of UNESCO's division of philosophy and humanistic studies. He is a member of the American Philosophical Association and the Church History Society, and a Fellow of the American Academy of Arts and Sciences.

Dr. Schneider co-edits the *Journal of Philosophy*, and among his books are *A History of American Philosophy*, *Religion in Twentieth Century America*, *Three Dimensions of Public Morality*, *The Puritan Mind*, *Making the Fascist State*, and *A Bibliography of John Dewey* (co-author).